Golf Training Log and Diary

This Book Belongs To:

_____

Visit http://elegantnotebooks.com for more sports training books.

Training Log and Diary
Nutrition Log and Diary
Strength and Conditioning Log and Diary

©Elegant Notebooks

DATE: _____ **WEEK:** _____ **HOURS TRAINED:** _____

INSTRUCTOR: _____ **TIME:** _____

GOALS

WARM UP/ DRILLS

TECHNIQUE 1

TECHNIQUE 2

NOTES

DATE: _____ **WEEK:** _____ **HOURS TRAINED:** _____

INSTRUCTOR: _____ **TIME:** _____

GOALS

WARM UP/ DRILLS

TECHNIQUE 1

TECHNIQUE 2

NOTES

DATE: [   ] **WEEK:** [   ] **HOURS TRAINED:** [   ]

INSTRUCTOR: [   ] **TIME:** [   ]

GOALS

WARM UP/ DRILLS

TECHNIQUE 1

TECHNIQUE 2

NOTES

DATE: **WEEK:** **HOURS TRAINED:**

INSTRUCTOR: **TIME:**

GOALS

WARM UP/ DRILLS

TECHNIQUE 1

TECHNIQUE 2

NOTES

DATE: **WEEK:**   **HOURS TRAINED:**

INSTRUCTOR: **TIME:**

GOALS

WARM UP/ DRILLS

TECHNIQUE 1

TECHNIQUE 2

NOTES

DATE: _____ **WEEK:** _____ **HOURS TRAINED:** _____

INSTRUCTOR: _____ **TIME:** _____

GOALS

WARM UP/ DRILLS

TECHNIQUE 1

TECHNIQUE 2

NOTES

DATE: [   ] **WEEK:** [   ] **HOURS TRAINED:** [   ]

INSTRUCTOR: [   ] **TIME:** [   ]

GOALS

WARM UP/ DRILLS

TECHNIQUE 1

TECHNIQUE 2

NOTES

DATE: **WEEK:** **HOURS TRAINED:**

INSTRUCTOR: **TIME:**

GOALS

WARM UP/ DRILLS

TECHNIQUE 1

TECHNIQUE 2

NOTES

DATE: | **WEEK:** | **HOURS TRAINED:**

INSTRUCTOR: | **TIME:**

GOALS

WARM UP/ DRILLS

TECHNIQUE 1

TECHNIQUE 2

NOTES

DATE: _____ **WEEK:** _____ **HOURS TRAINED:** _____

INSTRUCTOR: _____ **TIME:** _____

GOALS

WARM UP/ DRILLS

TECHNIQUE 1

TECHNIQUE 2

NOTES

DATE: **WEEK:**   **HOURS TRAINED:**

INSTRUCTOR: **TIME:**

GOALS

WARM UP/ DRILLS

TECHNIQUE 1

TECHNIQUE 2

NOTES

DATE: **WEEK:** **HOURS TRAINED:**

INSTRUCTOR: **TIME:**

GOALS

WARM UP/ DRILLS

TECHNIQUE 1

TECHNIQUE 2

NOTES

DATE: _____ **WEEK:** _____ **HOURS TRAINED:** _____

INSTRUCTOR: _____ **TIME:** _____

GOALS

WARM UP/ DRILLS

TECHNIQUE 1

TECHNIQUE 2

NOTES

DATE: _____ **WEEK:** _____ **HOURS TRAINED:** _____

INSTRUCTOR: _____ **TIME:** _____

GOALS

WARM UP/ DRILLS

TECHNIQUE 1

TECHNIQUE 2

NOTES

DATE: _____ **WEEK:** _____ **HOURS TRAINED:** _____

INSTRUCTOR: _____ **TIME:** _____

GOALS

WARM UP/ DRILLS

TECHNIQUE 1

TECHNIQUE 2

NOTES

DATE: **WEEK:** **HOURS TRAINED:**

INSTRUCTOR: **TIME:**

GOALS

WARM UP/ DRILLS

TECHNIQUE 1

TECHNIQUE 2

NOTES

DATE: **WEEK:** **HOURS TRAINED:**

INSTRUCTOR: **TIME:**

GOALS

WARM UP/ DRILLS

TECHNIQUE 1

TECHNIQUE 2

NOTES

DATE: **WEEK:** **HOURS TRAINED:**

INSTRUCTOR: **TIME:**

GOALS

WARM UP/ DRILLS

TECHNIQUE 1

TECHNIQUE 2

NOTES

DATE: _____ **WEEK:** _____ **HOURS TRAINED:** _____

INSTRUCTOR: _____ **TIME:** _____

GOALS

WARM UP/ DRILLS

TECHNIQUE 1

TECHNIQUE 2

NOTES

DATE: **WEEK:** **HOURS TRAINED:**

INSTRUCTOR: **TIME:**

GOALS

WARM UP/ DRILLS

TECHNIQUE 1

TECHNIQUE 2

NOTES

DATE: _____ **WEEK:** _____ **HOURS TRAINED:** _____

INSTRUCTOR: _____ **TIME:** _____

GOALS

WARM UP/ DRILLS

TECHNIQUE 1

TECHNIQUE 2

NOTES

DATE: _____ **WEEK:** _____ **HOURS TRAINED:** _____

INSTRUCTOR: _____ **TIME:** _____

GOALS

WARM UP/ DRILLS

TECHNIQUE 1

TECHNIQUE 2

NOTES

DATE: **WEEK:** **HOURS TRAINED:**

INSTRUCTOR: **TIME:**

GOALS

WARM UP/ DRILLS

TECHNIQUE 1

TECHNIQUE 2

NOTES

DATE: _____ **WEEK:** _____ **HOURS TRAINED:** _____

INSTRUCTOR: _____ **TIME:** _____

GOALS

WARM UP/ DRILLS

TECHNIQUE 1

TECHNIQUE 2

NOTES

DATE: _____ **WEEK:** _____ **HOURS TRAINED:** _____

INSTRUCTOR: _____ **TIME:** _____

GOALS

WARM UP/ DRILLS

TECHNIQUE 1

TECHNIQUE 2

NOTES

DATE: **WEEK:** **HOURS TRAINED:**

INSTRUCTOR: **TIME:**

GOALS

WARM UP/ DRILLS

TECHNIQUE 1

TECHNIQUE 2

NOTES

DATE: [   ] **WEEK:** [   ] **HOURS TRAINED:** [   ]

INSTRUCTOR: [   ] **TIME:** [   ]

GOALS

WARM UP/ DRILLS

TECHNIQUE 1

TECHNIQUE 2

NOTES

DATE: _____   **WEEK:** _____   **HOURS TRAINED:** _____

INSTRUCTOR: _____   **TIME:** _____

GOALS

WARM UP/ DRILLS

TECHNIQUE 1

TECHNIQUE 2

NOTES

DATE: | **WEEK:** | **HOURS TRAINED:**

INSTRUCTOR: | **TIME:**

GOALS

WARM UP/ DRILLS

TECHNIQUE 1

TECHNIQUE 2

NOTES

DATE: **WEEK:**   **HOURS TRAINED:**

INSTRUCTOR: **TIME:**

GOALS

WARM UP/ DRILLS

TECHNIQUE 1

TECHNIQUE 2

NOTES

DATE: _____ **WEEK:** _____ **HOURS TRAINED:** _____

INSTRUCTOR: _____ **TIME:** _____

GOALS

WARM UP/ DRILLS

TECHNIQUE 1

TECHNIQUE 2

NOTES

DATE: _____   **WEEK:** _____   **HOURS TRAINED:** _____

INSTRUCTOR: _____   **TIME:** _____

GOALS

WARM UP/ DRILLS

TECHNIQUE 1

TECHNIQUE 2

NOTES

DATE: _____ **WEEK:** _____ **HOURS TRAINED:** _____

INSTRUCTOR: _____ **TIME:** _____

GOALS

WARM UP/ DRILLS

TECHNIQUE 1

TECHNIQUE 2

NOTES

DATE: _____ **WEEK:** _____ **HOURS TRAINED:** _____

INSTRUCTOR: _____ **TIME:** _____

GOALS

WARM UP/ DRILLS

TECHNIQUE 1

TECHNIQUE 2

NOTES

DATE: **WEEK:** **HOURS TRAINED:**

INSTRUCTOR: **TIME:**

GOALS

WARM UP/ DRILLS

TECHNIQUE 1

TECHNIQUE 2

NOTES

DATE: **WEEK:** **HOURS TRAINED:**

INSTRUCTOR: **TIME:**

GOALS

WARM UP/ DRILLS

TECHNIQUE 1

TECHNIQUE 2

NOTES

DATE: _____ **WEEK:** _____ **HOURS TRAINED:** _____

INSTRUCTOR: _____ **TIME:** _____

GOALS

WARM UP/ DRILLS

TECHNIQUE 1

TECHNIQUE 2

NOTES

DATE: **WEEK:** **HOURS TRAINED:**

INSTRUCTOR: **TIME:**

GOALS

WARM UP/ DRILLS

TECHNIQUE 1

TECHNIQUE 2

NOTES

DATE: _____ **WEEK:** _____ **HOURS TRAINED:** _____

INSTRUCTOR: _____ **TIME:** _____

GOALS

WARM UP/ DRILLS

TECHNIQUE 1

TECHNIQUE 2

NOTES

DATE: **WEEK:** **HOURS TRAINED:**

INSTRUCTOR: **TIME:**

GOALS

WARM UP/ DRILLS

TECHNIQUE 1

TECHNIQUE 2

NOTES

DATE: _____ **WEEK:** _____ **HOURS TRAINED:** _____

INSTRUCTOR: _____ **TIME:** _____

GOALS

WARM UP/ DRILLS

TECHNIQUE 1

TECHNIQUE 2

NOTES

DATE: **WEEK:**   **HOURS TRAINED:**

INSTRUCTOR: **TIME:**

GOALS

WARM UP/ DRILLS

TECHNIQUE 1

TECHNIQUE 2

NOTES

DATE: **WEEK:**   **HOURS TRAINED:**

INSTRUCTOR: **TIME:**

GOALS

WARM UP/ DRILLS

TECHNIQUE 1

TECHNIQUE 2

NOTES

DATE: _____ **WEEK:** _____ **HOURS TRAINED:** _____

INSTRUCTOR: _____ **TIME:** _____

GOALS

WARM UP/ DRILLS

TECHNIQUE 1

TECHNIQUE 2

NOTES

DATE: [　　　　　] **WEEK:** [　　] **HOURS TRAINED:** [　　　　]

INSTRUCTOR: [　　　　　　　　　] **TIME:** [　　　　]

GOALS

WARM UP/ DRILLS

TECHNIQUE 1

TECHNIQUE 2

NOTES

DATE: _____ **WEEK:** _____ **HOURS TRAINED:** _____

INSTRUCTOR: _____ **TIME:** _____

GOALS

WARM UP/ DRILLS

TECHNIQUE 1

TECHNIQUE 2

NOTES

DATE: _____ **WEEK:** _____ **HOURS TRAINED:** _____

INSTRUCTOR: _____ **TIME:** _____

GOALS

WARM UP/ DRILLS

TECHNIQUE 1

TECHNIQUE 2

NOTES

DATE: _____ **WEEK:** _____ **HOURS TRAINED:** _____

INSTRUCTOR: _____ **TIME:** _____

GOALS

WARM UP/ DRILLS

TECHNIQUE 1

TECHNIQUE 2

NOTES

DATE: | **WEEK:** | **HOURS TRAINED:**

INSTRUCTOR: | **TIME:**

GOALS

WARM UP/ DRILLS

TECHNIQUE 1

TECHNIQUE 2

NOTES

DATE: _____ **WEEK:** _____ **HOURS TRAINED:** _____

INSTRUCTOR: _____ **TIME:** _____

GOALS

WARM UP/ DRILLS

TECHNIQUE 1

TECHNIQUE 2

NOTES

DATE: | **WEEK:** | **HOURS TRAINED:**

INSTRUCTOR: | **TIME:**

GOALS

WARM UP/ DRILLS

TECHNIQUE 1

TECHNIQUE 2

NOTES

DATE: **WEEK:**   **HOURS TRAINED:**

INSTRUCTOR: **TIME:**

GOALS

WARM UP/ DRILLS

TECHNIQUE 1

TECHNIQUE 2

NOTES

DATE: [　　　　　　] **WEEK:** [　　] **HOURS TRAINED:** [　　　　]

INSTRUCTOR: [　　　　　　　　　　] **TIME:** [　　　　]

GOALS

WARM UP/ DRILLS

TECHNIQUE 1

TECHNIQUE 2

NOTES

DATE: **WEEK:**   **HOURS TRAINED:**

INSTRUCTOR: **TIME:**

GOALS

WARM UP/ DRILLS

TECHNIQUE 1

TECHNIQUE 2

NOTES

DATE: _____ **WEEK:** _____ **HOURS TRAINED:** _____

INSTRUCTOR: _____ **TIME:** _____

GOALS

WARM UP/ DRILLS

TECHNIQUE 1

TECHNIQUE 2

NOTES

DATE: [   ] **WEEK:** [   ] **HOURS TRAINED:** [   ]

INSTRUCTOR: [   ] **TIME:** [   ]

GOALS

WARM UP/ DRILLS

TECHNIQUE 1

TECHNIQUE 2

NOTES

DATE: | **WEEK:** | **HOURS TRAINED:**

INSTRUCTOR: | **TIME:**

GOALS

WARM UP/ DRILLS

TECHNIQUE 1

TECHNIQUE 2

NOTES

DATE: **WEEK:**   **HOURS TRAINED:**

INSTRUCTOR: **TIME:**

GOALS

WARM UP/ DRILLS

TECHNIQUE 1

TECHNIQUE 2

NOTES

DATE: _____ **WEEK:** ____ **HOURS TRAINED:** _____

INSTRUCTOR: _____ **TIME:** _____

GOALS

WARM UP/ DRILLS

TECHNIQUE 1

TECHNIQUE 2

NOTES

DATE: _____ **WEEK:** _____ **HOURS TRAINED:** _____

INSTRUCTOR: _____ **TIME:** _____

GOALS

WARM UP/ DRILLS

TECHNIQUE 1

TECHNIQUE 2

NOTES

DATE: **WEEK:** **HOURS TRAINED:**

INSTRUCTOR: **TIME:**

GOALS

WARM UP/ DRILLS

TECHNIQUE 1

TECHNIQUE 2

NOTES

DATE: _____ **WEEK:** _____ **HOURS TRAINED:** _____

INSTRUCTOR: _____ **TIME:** _____

GOALS

WARM UP/ DRILLS

TECHNIQUE 1

TECHNIQUE 2

NOTES

DATE: **WEEK:**   **HOURS TRAINED:**

INSTRUCTOR: **TIME:**

GOALS

WARM UP/ DRILLS

TECHNIQUE 1

TECHNIQUE 2

NOTES

DATE: _____ **WEEK:** _____ **HOURS TRAINED:** _____

INSTRUCTOR: _____ **TIME:** _____

GOALS

WARM UP/ DRILLS

TECHNIQUE 1

TECHNIQUE 2

NOTES

DATE: [ ] **WEEK:** [ ] **HOURS TRAINED:** [ ]

INSTRUCTOR: [ ] **TIME:** [ ]

GOALS

WARM UP/ DRILLS

TECHNIQUE 1

TECHNIQUE 2

NOTES

DATE: _____ **WEEK:** _____ **HOURS TRAINED:** _____

INSTRUCTOR: _____ **TIME:** _____

GOALS

WARM UP/ DRILLS

TECHNIQUE 1

TECHNIQUE 2

NOTES

DATE: _____ **WEEK:** _____ **HOURS TRAINED:** _____

INSTRUCTOR: _____ **TIME:** _____

GOALS

WARM UP/ DRILLS

TECHNIQUE 1

TECHNIQUE 2

NOTES

DATE: **WEEK:**   **HOURS TRAINED:**

INSTRUCTOR: **TIME:**

GOALS

WARM UP/ DRILLS

TECHNIQUE 1

TECHNIQUE 2

NOTES

DATE: _____ **WEEK:** _____ **HOURS TRAINED:** _____

INSTRUCTOR: _____ **TIME:** _____

GOALS

WARM UP/ DRILLS

TECHNIQUE 1

TECHNIQUE 2

NOTES

DATE: _____ **WEEK:** ____ **HOURS TRAINED:** _____

INSTRUCTOR: _____ **TIME:** _____

GOALS

WARM UP/ DRILLS

TECHNIQUE 1

TECHNIQUE 2

NOTES

DATE: _____ **WEEK:** _____ **HOURS TRAINED:** _____

INSTRUCTOR: _____ **TIME:** _____

GOALS

WARM UP/ DRILLS

TECHNIQUE 1

TECHNIQUE 2

NOTES

DATE: **WEEK:**   **HOURS TRAINED:**

INSTRUCTOR: **TIME:**

GOALS

WARM UP/ DRILLS

TECHNIQUE 1

TECHNIQUE 2

NOTES

DATE: **WEEK:** **HOURS TRAINED:**

INSTRUCTOR: **TIME:**

GOALS

WARM UP/ DRILLS

TECHNIQUE 1

TECHNIQUE 2

NOTES

DATE: _____ **WEEK:** _____ **HOURS TRAINED:** _____

INSTRUCTOR: _____ **TIME:** _____

GOALS

WARM UP/ DRILLS

TECHNIQUE 1

TECHNIQUE 2

NOTES

DATE: | **WEEK:** | **HOURS TRAINED:**

INSTRUCTOR: | **TIME:**

GOALS

WARM UP/ DRILLS

TECHNIQUE 1

TECHNIQUE 2

NOTES

DATE: _____ **WEEK:** _____ **HOURS TRAINED:** _____

INSTRUCTOR: _____ **TIME:** _____

GOALS

WARM UP/ DRILLS

TECHNIQUE 1

TECHNIQUE 2

NOTES

DATE: **WEEK:** **HOURS TRAINED:**

INSTRUCTOR: **TIME:**

GOALS

WARM UP/ DRILLS

TECHNIQUE 1

TECHNIQUE 2

NOTES

DATE: **WEEK:** **HOURS TRAINED:**

INSTRUCTOR: **TIME:**

GOALS

WARM UP/ DRILLS

TECHNIQUE 1

TECHNIQUE 2

NOTES

DATE: _____   **WEEK:** _____   **HOURS TRAINED:** _____

INSTRUCTOR: _____   **TIME:** _____

GOALS

WARM UP/ DRILLS

TECHNIQUE 1

TECHNIQUE 2

NOTES

DATE: [ ]   WEEK: [ ]   HOURS TRAINED: [ ]

INSTRUCTOR: [ ]   TIME: [ ]

GOALS

WARM UP/ DRILLS

TECHNIQUE 1

TECHNIQUE 2

NOTES

DATE: _____ **WEEK:** _____ **HOURS TRAINED:** _____

INSTRUCTOR: _____ **TIME:** _____

GOALS

WARM UP/ DRILLS

TECHNIQUE 1

TECHNIQUE 2

NOTES

DATE: _____ **WEEK:** _____ **HOURS TRAINED:** _____

INSTRUCTOR: _____ **TIME:** _____

GOALS

WARM UP/ DRILLS

TECHNIQUE 1

TECHNIQUE 2

NOTES

DATE: _____ **WEEK:** _____ **HOURS TRAINED:** _____

INSTRUCTOR: _____ **TIME:** _____

GOALS

WARM UP/ DRILLS

TECHNIQUE 1

TECHNIQUE 2

NOTES

DATE: _____ **WEEK:** _____ **HOURS TRAINED:** _____

INSTRUCTOR: _____ **TIME:** _____

GOALS

WARM UP/ DRILLS

TECHNIQUE 1

TECHNIQUE 2

NOTES

DATE: **WEEK:** **HOURS TRAINED:**

INSTRUCTOR: **TIME:**

GOALS

WARM UP/ DRILLS

TECHNIQUE 1

TECHNIQUE 2

NOTES

DATE: _____ **WEEK:** _____ **HOURS TRAINED:** _____

INSTRUCTOR: _____ **TIME:** _____

GOALS

WARM UP/ DRILLS

TECHNIQUE 1

TECHNIQUE 2

NOTES

DATE: | **WEEK:** | **HOURS TRAINED:**

INSTRUCTOR: | **TIME:**

GOALS

WARM UP/ DRILLS

TECHNIQUE 1

TECHNIQUE 2

NOTES

DATE: **WEEK:** **HOURS TRAINED:**

INSTRUCTOR: **TIME:**

GOALS

WARM UP/ DRILLS

TECHNIQUE 1

TECHNIQUE 2

NOTES

DATE: **WEEK:**   **HOURS TRAINED:**

INSTRUCTOR: **TIME:**

GOALS

WARM UP/ DRILLS

TECHNIQUE 1

TECHNIQUE 2

NOTES

DATE: _____ **WEEK:** _____ **HOURS TRAINED:** _____

INSTRUCTOR: _____ **TIME:** _____

GOALS

WARM UP/ DRILLS

TECHNIQUE 1

TECHNIQUE 2

NOTES

DATE: **WEEK:** **HOURS TRAINED:**

INSTRUCTOR: **TIME:**

GOALS

WARM UP/ DRILLS

TECHNIQUE 1

TECHNIQUE 2

NOTES

DATE: | **WEEK:** | **HOURS TRAINED:**

INSTRUCTOR: | **TIME:**

GOALS

WARM UP/ DRILLS

TECHNIQUE 1

TECHNIQUE 2

NOTES

DATE: **WEEK:** **HOURS TRAINED:**

INSTRUCTOR: **TIME:**

GOALS

WARM UP/ DRILLS

TECHNIQUE 1

TECHNIQUE 2

NOTES

DATE: _____ **WEEK:** _____ **HOURS TRAINED:** _____

INSTRUCTOR: _____ **TIME:** _____

GOALS

WARM UP/ DRILLS

TECHNIQUE 1

TECHNIQUE 2

NOTES

DATE: **WEEK:**   **HOURS TRAINED:**

INSTRUCTOR: **TIME:**

GOALS

WARM UP/ DRILLS

TECHNIQUE 1

TECHNIQUE 2

NOTES

DATE: _____ **WEEK:** _____ **HOURS TRAINED:** _____

INSTRUCTOR: _____ **TIME:** _____

GOALS

WARM UP/ DRILLS

TECHNIQUE 1

TECHNIQUE 2

NOTES

DATE: [   ]   **WEEK:** [   ]   **HOURS TRAINED:** [   ]

INSTRUCTOR: [   ]   **TIME:** [   ]

GOALS

WARM UP/ DRILLS

TECHNIQUE 1

TECHNIQUE 2

NOTES

DATE: _____ **WEEK:** _____ **HOURS TRAINED:** _____

INSTRUCTOR: _____ **TIME:** _____

GOALS

WARM UP/ DRILLS

TECHNIQUE 1

TECHNIQUE 2

NOTES

DATE: **WEEK:**   **HOURS TRAINED:**

INSTRUCTOR: **TIME:**

GOALS

WARM UP/ DRILLS

TECHNIQUE 1

TECHNIQUE 2

NOTES

DATE: **WEEK:** **HOURS TRAINED:**

INSTRUCTOR: **TIME:**

GOALS

WARM UP/ DRILLS

TECHNIQUE 1

TECHNIQUE 2

NOTES

DATE: _____ **WEEK:** _____ **HOURS TRAINED:** _____

INSTRUCTOR: _____ **TIME:** _____

GOALS

WARM UP/ DRILLS

TECHNIQUE 1

TECHNIQUE 2

NOTES

DATE: **WEEK:** **HOURS TRAINED:**

INSTRUCTOR: **TIME:**

GOALS

WARM UP/ DRILLS

TECHNIQUE 1

TECHNIQUE 2

NOTES

DATE: _____ **WEEK:** _____ **HOURS TRAINED:** _____

INSTRUCTOR: _____ **TIME:** _____

GOALS

WARM UP/ DRILLS

TECHNIQUE 1

TECHNIQUE 2

NOTES

DATE: _____ **WEEK:** _____ **HOURS TRAINED:** _____

INSTRUCTOR: _____ **TIME:** _____

GOALS

WARM UP/ DRILLS

TECHNIQUE 1

TECHNIQUE 2

NOTES

DATE: **WEEK:**   **HOURS TRAINED:**

INSTRUCTOR: **TIME:**

GOALS

WARM UP/ DRILLS

TECHNIQUE 1

TECHNIQUE 2

NOTES

DATE: **WEEK:** **HOURS TRAINED:**

INSTRUCTOR: **TIME:**

GOALS

WARM UP/ DRILLS

TECHNIQUE 1

TECHNIQUE 2

NOTES

DATE: [   ]   **WEEK:** [   ]   **HOURS TRAINED:** [   ]

INSTRUCTOR: [   ]   **TIME:** [   ]

GOALS

WARM UP/ DRILLS

TECHNIQUE 1

TECHNIQUE 2

NOTES

DATE: _____ **WEEK:** _____ **HOURS TRAINED:** _____

INSTRUCTOR: _____ **TIME:** _____

GOALS

WARM UP/ DRILLS

TECHNIQUE 1

TECHNIQUE 2

NOTES

DATE: **WEEK:** **HOURS TRAINED:**

INSTRUCTOR: **TIME:**

GOALS

WARM UP/ DRILLS

TECHNIQUE 1

TECHNIQUE 2

NOTES

DATE: _____ **WEEK:** _____ **HOURS TRAINED:** _____

INSTRUCTOR: _____ **TIME:** _____

GOALS

WARM UP/ DRILLS

TECHNIQUE 1

TECHNIQUE 2

NOTES

DATE: | **WEEK:** | **HOURS TRAINED:**

INSTRUCTOR: | **TIME:**

GOALS

WARM UP/ DRILLS

TECHNIQUE 1

TECHNIQUE 2

NOTES

DATE: _____ **WEEK:** _____ **HOURS TRAINED:** _____

INSTRUCTOR: _____ **TIME:** _____

GOALS

WARM UP/ DRILLS

TECHNIQUE 1

TECHNIQUE 2

NOTES

DATE: **WEEK:**   **HOURS TRAINED:**

INSTRUCTOR: **TIME:**

GOALS

WARM UP/ DRILLS

TECHNIQUE 1

TECHNIQUE 2

NOTES

DATE: WEEK: HOURS TRAINED:

INSTRUCTOR: TIME:

GOALS

WARM UP/ DRILLS

TECHNIQUE 1

TECHNIQUE 2

NOTES

DATE: | **WEEK:** | **HOURS TRAINED:**

INSTRUCTOR: | **TIME:**

GOALS

WARM UP/ DRILLS

TECHNIQUE 1

TECHNIQUE 2

NOTES

DATE: **WEEK:**   **HOURS TRAINED:**

INSTRUCTOR: **TIME:**

GOALS

WARM UP/ DRILLS

TECHNIQUE 1

TECHNIQUE 2

NOTES

DATE: _____ **WEEK:** _____ **HOURS TRAINED:** _____

INSTRUCTOR: _____ **TIME:** _____

GOALS

WARM UP/ DRILLS

TECHNIQUE 1

TECHNIQUE 2

NOTES

DATE: **WEEK:**   **HOURS TRAINED:**

INSTRUCTOR: **TIME:**

GOALS

WARM UP/ DRILLS

TECHNIQUE 1

TECHNIQUE 2

NOTES

DATE: **WEEK:** **HOURS TRAINED:**

INSTRUCTOR: **TIME:**

GOALS

WARM UP/ DRILLS

TECHNIQUE 1

TECHNIQUE 2

NOTES

Printed in Great Britain
by Amazon